VOICES

POETRY BY WAC ARTS COLLEGE

Taking as a starting point the legal battle of former Lauderdale resident William Mead in 1670 for religious tolerance and a fair trial, the young people from Wac Arts College explored the power of poetry to respond to issues that were important to them such as racism, gender and education. Led by Anthony Anaxagorou, young people crafted poems and explored poetic theory to better use the power of words to express their point of view. This has resulted in some moving and inspirational poetry.

This project was possible thanks to funding from Heritage Lottery Fund and John Lyon's Charity.

Maddy Gilliam
Heritage Education Officer
Lauderdale House

The work created over a period of six weeks explores what it means to be human by looking at a series of fundamental human rights - the right to self-identity, to self-determine and to live a full life without fear of violence or persecution. The poems found in this collection were borne of discussions around all of the above. The students unpacked and wrestled with the many ways our lives and the lives of others can be affected by law, policy, civil unrest and mercurial cultural standards.

We looked at how art can provide a fresh way to look at these issues and spent our hour each week refining a language which best fit each sentiment and experience.

Anthony Anaxagorou
Writer of poetry, fiction and prose.
Artistic director of Out-Spoken and publisher at Out-Spoken Press

VOICES

The Fingerprint of Nothingness

Sandra Neves Sousa
Post 16 Student

She said you can't touch my blood
My identity
The genes I know were handed down to me

She said you can't touch my blood
This is how I save lives
must we all sacrifice

She said you can't touch my blood
Because this connects me to my family
A life I know where centuries of history flow through

She said you can only touch my blood
When you see the life I bring to this world
You can only touch my blood
When you hear the way I leave this world

She said you can't touch my blood
Because it's part of a temple that grows inside
containing secrets and knowledge only my mind
can breathe only I hold the key to the cabinets
Without my blood there is nothing
Therefore you cannot identify me

Red Queen

Michelle Murray
Learning Support Assistant

You can't touch my mind,
a monastery, sanctuary of peace
a city on fire, frozen summit

Worlds within worlds, vastness
the deep wilderness, the dark growth,
fecundity would amaze you

down the rabbit hole
to the land of the red queen,
while the mad hatter sways
his internal song of insanity
turned inward

of friends there are enemies
who offend
the silent voice commanding imagination
the knowledge acquired from years of solace,

depths hidden away from you

laughing at the idea that you think you know
the space between my sanctuary.

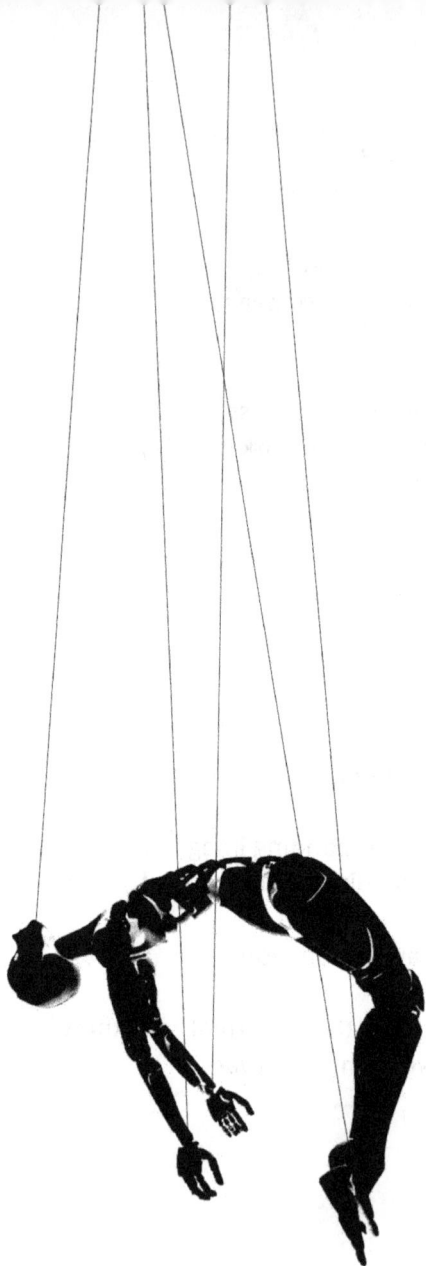

Puppeteer

Carlo Chirila
Post 16 Student

When I look at the sky, the sea, the mountains,
the green, the purity of such places
I wonder how something can be so perfect
and yet so vulnerable.
I wonder if that's the reality of another dream
made for us to believe,
made from the man of the machines.
Pulling strings. Making streams of blood and tears
for those things which we need and helps us live
or to be more real I'd say we need those things
in order for us to live.

When I look at man, I see potential, I see progression,
he could be great and free yet he lacks something,
something which defines what human is.

What makes us human, is the love
and being able to understand as well as communicate to create.

Selfishness took the lead of this world
falling in greed and in meaningless emotions covered up
by masks of sorrow which leads to a horrible
and constructed tomorrow.

Looking at kids giving away themselves for these puppets
led by this revolting puppeteer made of poison,
the same man you call politician,
the same man that turned us into machines,
the same man that created greed, the same man birthing wars
the same man that took your freedom to be
the Man you always wanted to be.

The Garden Path

Elijah Hammond Dallas

Learning support assistant

You can't touch my past
My lonely, unfinished path.
Carved from lessons of my mother tongue and mother one.
Weaving past time thorns
Guided by timeworn trees,
Still so green to me.
Enabling me to breathe easily.
I can't touch my past, it resides in my lungs
Left with the young leaves.
The quiet kid with the afro.
Locked in a photograph

You can't touch the past scars, they've faded.
Past tears dried
Laughter now quiet. Frowns forgotten.
You can't touch my past, Only I can properly forget and
remember
Can't be stored
Won't be destroyed
Seen or unseen.
It's buried deep in the clouds
Lie on the grass
Watch past pass.

One Word About Everything

Joely Harris-Tharp
Post 16 Student

We were humans until race disconnected us
Things all around, wanting to create,
A world that isn't filled with hate.

Frustrated minds scream for release
Whether you're black or white
It's only a colour.
Help one another rather than criticise.

In a so called democracy.
Racism happens beyond the theory
Here where we scream black lives matter
I'm not racist, my sisters boyfriend's black
I'm not racist, my cousins girlfriend's black.

The gun in the word nigger
The word puts us under our graves
When we say that it's just how we say hi to each other
Greeting us dead.

There are two skies in every story
I'd only want to exist peacefully in mine.

Untethered

Chanel Sabrah
Student

You can't touch my vessel, it holds all my demons. A simple scratch will send one out sneaking through the wound.

You can't touch my vessel, you've got blood on your hands. They'll smell it through my pores, scratch at the back of my eyelids, gnawing beneath my skin.

Every time you advance closer one will break from it's rusted chains, limping, dropping, crawling, heaving, foaming, nails digging into the soil killing whatever thoughts were ready to harvest.

Do not touch my vessel, the minute you hold me, I'll skip from your embrace and shatter, like the cheeks of a porcelain doll from the top shelf.

My untethered soul will scream in frequencies that human ears cannot fathom, causing delicate minds to hallucinate in colours undiscovered.

It'll be me left glueing my pieces together to hold what's left. But, do I want to anymore? My demons will soar out of my lifeless body one by one revealing their truths like a sinner at confession.

Forgive me father for I am about to sin.

continued over the page...

Anxiety will cower in a corner reciting your name like a prayer. Pain will cling to your feet, nails digging at your dermis, beads of blood form and drip like tapped syrup from a maple tree. Sadness will hang itself weeping above your head,

drenching you in toxic tears eating away your clothes leaving you exposed with the stench of poisonous petrichor.

My energies all unbalanced will torment what's left of your soul. Anger will claw at your confidence and break you into pieces. Love will beg for your forgiveness for it will hopelessly believe you deserved what it gave you.

Care will clean at your wounds and kiss your tear stained cheeks. I'm not a narcissist for saying only a certain people can handle me, I'm still broken.

Do not touch my vessel I still have no control.

You won't touch my vessel You simply don't know how.

A Swerve in our Knowledge

Angel Lema
Post 16 Student

The constriction was so patronising that even the authority became aware.

The pages crinkled, deteriorated as did the clock's dull hum. The withheld knowledge bounced off the walls, asking, praying, begging for a captor. DNA copies ponder the surroundings, gripping tightly

to what once was, what should still be.

Ghost feelings to reminisce in. Untold realities craving someone to delve,

someone to jump, someone to trust. A thought, a process, a chair, a completion,

a child that asks for just a minute of your time that you brush away

with the wave of a hand, the brain of an ignorant,

because he probably will grow up and be like you.

Only then, in the midst of a carbon copy generation, you'll be scared.

Only then you'll see the problem. Make amends with your past,

because history repeats itself and sometimes, for blame's sake,

we ignore that one wrong turn.

Creative Writing Project

Our writing sessions produced a diverse community of writers, who wrote scripts, short stories, and poetry from a variety of genres. From alien creatures in Hawaii, to rap lyrics inspired by Macbeth, the students created exciting narratives. The poems featured here are from our last session. The students were asked to write a postcard poem to someone they found inspiring or to their future selves.

Chibeza Mumbi
Creative Writing Tutor

To Future Rebecca, with Love

Rebecca Hannett
Post 16 Student

Keep being yourself.
Don't let the paparazzi overwhelm you,
always keep in contact with all
your old friends and family.

Don't let anyone in the industry,
change who you are
or tell you what to do or what to wear.

I hope you are still funny
and that your humour
comes across in your acting.

I hope you get along with your co-stars
even if working with them is hard.
Be grateful to the people
who helped you on your journey.

Teacher

Danny Lopes
Post 16 Student

With the love and joy that you give,
you are like a dove.
We all enjoy the way that you forgive.

Sometimes we shove
sometimes we destroy.
Now you will live
with the beautiful wings
that the lord hath give.

Not to forget about you Jarren,
you really do make me sweat
I cherish all the lessons
that I will never forget.

It's time to say goodbye,
all the love
I will give,
with the hate
I will always forgive.

Muhammad Ali

Joe Woolford
Post 16 Student

I am here to state why
you have inspired me over the years,
your most memorable moments.

You have shown great achievement
in your career,
which gave me so much inspiration.

You have shown me not to give in to anything
no matter what people say.

You have chosen to follow your dreams
and ignore the ones that told you
that you could not do it.

You fought with passion
and now look at your success,
you have taught me hard work pays off.

You have shown me what I can do
when I feel isolated.

You have shown me how to pursue things
when people tell you you are not good enough,
you need to try your hardest no matter what.

Martin Luther King

Jaydon Gosling Morgan
Pre 16 Student

As a young child, I was always inspired about what you did.
If it wasn't for you
I wouldn't have any non-black friends,
I'm so thankful for what you did.
It has helped me get to know many more people,
and the world would not be so multicultural,
if you did not do what you did.

Ali

Yoonis Warsame
Post 16 Student

You're a legend,
mentor,
guide
and a man who fought
for human rights.

That tested the law,
when people thought
it would be impossible,
to question the authority and demand
justice for people.

That in general
gives the youth
that push
to challenge the law.

Wac Arts College provides alternative education for 14-19 year olds through a creative arts and media curriculum. The school consolidates over thirty years' experience of using arts and media education to turn disengaged young peoples' lives around. Our ethos is founded on a number of principles that are embedded through our work in non-statutory arts and media education.

We believe passionately that learning can—and should—be enjoyable. A creative curriculum puts pleasure back into learning, particularly if you have been alienated from or excluded by 'traditional' and 'mainstream' statutory education. Avoiding and resisting learning in school can often be signs of imagination and creativity. Many young people in alternative education are especially well suited for a career in the creative industries.

Wac Arts College, 213 Haverstock Hill, London NW3 4QP
Tel: 020 7692 5860 Email: info@WacArtsCollege.co.uk
www.WacArtsCollege.co.uk